Rhyme Rhythm Reason

More than Some of the Sum of My Poems

Paul Drakeford

Copyright © 2019 by Paul Drakeford.

All rights reserved. No part of this book may be reproduced or transmitted in any form or by any means, electronic or mechanical, including photocopying, recording, or by any information storage and retrieval system, without permission in writing from the copyright owner.

Any people depicted in stock imagery provided by Getty Images are models, and such images are being used for illustrative purposes only.
Certain stock imagery © Getty Images.

Contents

Foreword iii

The Broken Soul 1
When is a poet a poet? 3
To the Editor of *Overland* 5
Penny for a Piper 7
Souvenir 9
The Lemon Tree 11
Song of the South Australian Railways 13
The Renaissance 15
Poor Marianne 17
Life is a lonely planet 19
Lullaby 21
Morpheus aroused 23
Man is a Misfit 25
A Knight at the Baths 27
Making Shaw 31
The Trouble with Ants 37
The three monkeys 39

Foreword

Long ago
and yesterday,
from time to time
and one by one,
these orphan poems
came unannounced
to my front door
in search of names
to give them birth.

I brought them in,
gave them a home,
and set them down
to rest between
leaves of A4.

I thought perhaps
they'd be content
to sleep like heroes
from the war
but as years passed,
their restlessness
has grown to pitch
I can't ignore.

I send them out
then in the world
in hope some others
find them space,
adopt them as
one might a pet—
or even two—
to make best friends.

If misbehaviour
should occur, then
send them back
and no offence.
I will allow
their parentage
is quite obscure,
their genes awry;
they may present
unsocial ends.

And I may find
to my regret
they left a void
was cavalier
to generate.

No matter now.
What's done is done.
We share the risk
and they the fun.

The Broken Soul

The same—but oh so different.
To think that two score years ago,
I wandered as a child within this
Selfsame wood and found
Within its depth
Peace, life and beauty.

And now I gaze upon this everlasting scene
With these same eyes, grown wise
By life torn into shreds by war.
Through battle, deaths, and victories
It stretched until it parted.

And now I see, indeed in different light,
A murky wood of trees with
Outstretched arms of greed,
Clawing the air with hopes
Of finding power.
Their neighbours
Overrule the rest, as kings do slaves.

I see within that yonder sickly oak,
A poor man striving for his rights,
But all the while his lords do
Overshadow him, so he must die.
I goad my mind away from these cruel thoughts
And wend my way towards my lodging house.

(First published at the age of sixteen in my school magazine,
The Western Wyvern, November 1948.)

When is a poet a poet?

When is a poet a poet
is as wide and as weakly wise
as why is a crooked letter.

One swallow doesn't make a summer,
nor two limericks a bard.
One winter comes
and spring sings
love's sweet sorrows?.

Perhaps a ream of rhymes
might raise
a scribbler
to Parnassus.
A miscellany
of elevating elegies
might win the prize
and earn a crown
with gloss upon it.

What sum of sonnets
might atone
for poetastry?
Unless,
as some profess,
less is more,
and more is less.

When is a poet a poet?
Poetically,
when other poets
know it.

To the Editor of Overland
Stephen Murray-Smith

The publishing of poesy
Life completes.
But in your specious case,
Refer to Keats.

You sway about upon a rocking horse
Called Pegasus.
Thus take us for a ride,
Which all but beggars us.

You proffer punctuation,
Bits of parquetry,
And reckon we're so dim
To think it's poetry.

And then Lord starve the crows.
And what is worse,
You publish lines of prose
And call it verse.

Alas, poor Stephen,
Rise up from your grave.
The typists in the office
Misbehave.

Penny for a Piper

The heat dripped heavy on the town,
like honey
lazy spilling from the sky-jar down
on roof and roadway, where it spread and oozed
with sticky, sickly heat.

"It's hot," said Mrs. Up-John.
"I will ring the mayor and tell him
that it's well within his ken to keep us cool."

She did,
and this is what he said.

"Madam, I will pay a penny
for a piper if you find that
you can name me any

who will pipe you rolling and a-rollick
down the highways of the land,
down the freeways
to the coolways,
to the sea,

where the slow sea silk
curls and crinkles on the beach,
and sea reeds ripple on the wind
and rave a paean of lucid coolness
to the ice-blue sky.

For a penny I would buy you magic
could you name an apt musician."

But Mrs. Up-John cut him off
and turned to Mrs. Beetle-Wise
with hell's hot judgement
on her lips.

"That man's a fool,"
she said.

(Published in *An Overland muster.* Brisbane: Jacaranda Press, 1965.)

Souvenir

"All visitors must now leave the ship."

This brittle moment to embrace
ends meeting,
sparks bright surprise
as eyes seek parting eyes.

The sum of this division
is expressed as
x minus y equals less.

Could this be the answer
to some problem yet proposed?

Store this solution then
this side up,
upstairs
in a damp-proof
drawer.

The Lemon Tree

I had a little lemon tree,
And nothing would it bear
But a yellow lemon,
And that was rather rare.

The King of Spain's daughter
Came to visit me.

"So where's this silver nutmeg
And my golden pear?"

"Just hold it there Girl.
You must have nuts in your head.
Can't you see I'm trying
To write a poem about a lemon tree?"

"Oh, I do beg your pardon,"
She hoity-toityly rejoindered.

"Yes, and beggars can't be choosers,"
I shot back.
That metaphorical flying sceptre
Got her right between the orbs.

"You might be royal,
But you're rude.
And you have no rhythm
And no rhyme.

And what's more,
You have the wrong address.
The nut tree is two doors down."

Off she flounced
And was never seen again.

Now where was I?
Oh yes.

I had a pair of nut trees ...

Oh bugger! I've lost the plot.

Song of the South Australian Railways

Gentlemen are requested
to refrain from passing urine
while the train is standing
in the station, please.

No smoking in the corridors,
the dining car, the lavatories.
No riding on the footplates
or the roof, and should you sneeze,

then use the place provided,
which is always at the other end,
located where the notices
say, Warning to all passengers,
and, Penalties for breaking
regulations such as these.

No expectoration, fornication,
procrastination, jubilation,
hibernation, altercation,
touching ladies' knees.

No hiccupping or hobbling
or swivelling or wobbling
or hurrying or coddling.

And most of all—

NO TRAVELLING!

(Originally published in Overland, no. 22, December 1961.)

The Renaissance

Miss Rafferty
put all her cast-off clothes
in a ragbag
and left them on the stoop.

The ragman
was to come next day
and take them off
to charitable industry.

But Mrs. Moggs upstairs
came rummaging
and found
a petticoat for Brenda,
a spencer hardly worn,
and stockings;
just the thing
for hanging woollies.

A wash and rinse
in case,
and out they went
to flutter in the air.

Miss Rafferty returned
to find the line
alive with memories.

Nothing had changed
except their ownership
and mystery.

(A true story recalled from about 1956.)

Poor Marianne

A Terrible, Tawdry Tale
of Love's Labours Lost

Marianne collected boys
As other girls collected toys.
She kept them in a special box,
In separate drawers with special locks.
At night she'd take one out to play,
And in the morning, lock away.
One toy boy she considered best.
In lower drawers she kept the rest.
She thought perhaps one day they'd wed
And buy themselves a feather bed.
She wasn't sure that he'd decide
To make her his beloved bride.
So rather put him to the test,
She bedded down the second best.
Alas! She waited far too long.
Her darling fled and did her wrong.
In desperation then she tried
To make herself a bartered bride.
But all her swains had picked the locks
And fled the scene in just their socks.
Abandoned thus and hopeless, too,
She'd no idea what to do.
And having languished in the lurch,
In desperation joined the church.
Her marriage race so badly run,
She missed her moment in the sun.
So sympathise with Marianne,
Who finished up an also-ran.

Life is a lonely planet

Life is a lonely planet,
where continental drift
severs connections.

Vast, wandering islands
carry us far and wide
at such a lack of pace
we shall be dust
ere continents collide.

Will sands of time
record our first conjunction?
Will sedimentary rocks
preserve the rift of us apart?
Or will erupt volcanoes mock
forgotten sorrows?

Earth tectonics has no need of sentiment.

Life is a lonely planet,
where strangers permanently
stand and stare
and wave
interminable
goodbyes.

Lullaby

Now go to sleep, my boy.
The day has been so long.
And while you sleep, my boy,
I'll sing you this sweet song.

I loved you through the day.
I'll love you through the night.
And in the morning time you'll find
I'm here to hold you tight.

So go to sleep, my boy.
The day has been so long.
And while you sleep, my boy,
I'll sing you this sweet song.

I loved you through the day,
And till the night is done.
And in the morning time, you'll smile.
So sleep, sweet sleep, my son.

Morpheus aroused

The telephone
nerve ends
at midnight
sleep alarms.

"Hello?"

Could this be him?
A mind with muscles
and a grin
to dream on?
A jockstrap on a PhD?
A prince priapic
with a red MG?

I wonder will he come to tea.,

"Can I speak to Cindy Lou?"

"May you speak to Cindy who?"
A moment's silence.

"Cindy Lou."

"Cindy Lou went slightly mad.
The things she did were very bad.
She frothed at the mouth
and wet the bed.
She wouldn't do a thing we said.
She wouldn't wear her dressing gown.
We had to put the creature down."

Then, "Oh …"

The penny drops.

"You clown!"

Another …

very wrong …

number.

Man is a Misfit

Man is a misfit.

Bigger than his size,
See him touch the skies,
While lesser lives
Are trampled to defeat.

All dies.

Then funeral fires
And priestly cries
Advise there is a God.
That God is man,
That men are gods,
All licensed to abuse.

All man's works offend,
And at his end,
Even his Earth
He'll bend
And break.

Man is a misfit,
Fit but to fail
And fall.

A Knight at the Baths

Chaste from the spa,
I must not fail.
My quest the gleaming
holy grail.

Heaven's above,
the glory whole,
the promised land of love.

Muzak on the stairs
is musk with mystery men.

The organ stirs.
The organ swells.

Should I descend?
Too late for terror.

Shall I pretend
sophisticate?

Did I ascend
a step too far?

No matter.
Kismet will defend
serenity.

This is the landing.
This is the final turn.
Dark corridor
where instincts burn.

A brushed thigh
sighs,
"Surprise. Surprise."
as eyes meet eyes.

What shadows these,
erect
and palely loitering at ease?

Can I identify
an avenue of angels?
an honour guard of ghouls?
a spring of rustlers?
or a pounce of common senses?

Too late.
All roams lead to Rhodes
and no return.
All ways lead to rooms
and no return.

Suppose they clutch on
my escutcheon,
will chinks in
shining armour
see me through?

Come gird my loins,
the battle beckons.
The jousts begin
and much to do.

A leather bed of wrestlers
lies within,
a restless sleep
of men at arms,
a love knot writhe
of arms and men.

No foes are found
as fond as these.

And suddenly
I'm taken in
and tumble down to
sense unseen.
My best defences
all undone.

No use the struggle
but consumed
with forces passions
might explain.

My youth laid waste
by sweaty swains
no champions these
of chivalry.

The kiss of kindness
I defend
till valour mete
their sorry end.

Thrice beat them off.
My wrath might forge
my rod for Harry
Edward and Sweet George

Unequal contest.
I resile.
A cry for help perhaps?
Or smile?

Succour my lords!
You are too hard.
I sue for peace.
There's ought to guard.

But soft
no whisper now
and not this night.

Tomorrow's fit
for panics and alarms.

Tonight
I am a knight
in arms.

Published in *Fourth dimensional kisses*. –Melbourne: Pampered Princess Publishing, 2003

Making Shaw

◆

He had the habit of mixing business with pleasure. He would read in the toilet. And if the reading were cerebrally stimulating, he could in time become fundamentally numbed.

He was more than halfway through *The Mammoth book of gay short stories*.

"A gay vampire? How bizarre! Well. A clever idea but ...

Now, what's next? *Prostitution* by Aiden Shaw. Aiden Shaw? That must be a rather common name. There's an Aiden Shaw in *Grease guns*, and a very upstanding young man at that."

He turned to the back pages for a thumbnail bio.

'Aiden Shaw is a porn movie star and prostitute, poet and performer and author of the novel Brutal. *He lives in London, England.'*

The same! He almost fell off his perch. He read on. The story, such as it was a story, consisted of excerpts from the story of a life as a callboy. Interesting. Fluent. Well written. Constructed. Politically incorrect. Probing. Stimulating. Brilliant.

He was warming to Aiden Shaw.

"This guy's more than just a hot number."

And he wondered in what other video heavens this star had sparkled. The only other he could immediately recall was *Command performance*, full of black Bechsteins. This was a job for an expert, a porn broker. He would ring his friend Bernie.

At the gym he remembered those grey eyes, that rose tattoo, segue to precious orbs, those strong thighs, that curving sti ...

"My my! I think I'm in love."

He was certainly swelling with more passion than pride. He decided to think instead about lat pull downs.

He rang his friend Bernie.

"Aiden Shaw? I'll just check my records." And then "Well he's in the *Adam video guides*" and he began to read the list. There were so many. *Black leather, Danger alley, Hot pursuit, Night force.* The list went on and on. Almost thirty titles. This Aiden Shaw certainly had some accomplishment under his belt, something to be proud of.

"Bernie I'm sure I'm in love."

"Well he doesn't do all that much for me."

So much the better. One fewer in the queue.

****

The tyranny of distance mitigates against profitable hanky waving. How was he to attract attention so far? Perhaps he could write a poem, compose a song. B flat. His favourite key.

Aiden
always comes before Baden
and I'd never trade Aiden
for Hayden.

Or perhaps

Play your cards right with Aiden
there's a laid down misère to be made in
diamonds and spades you could trade in.

"Needs a bit of work."

Perhaps a letter would be more appropriate. But what address? Well the publisher's would do. 7 Kensington Church Court. And what better place for serious romance than a Church Court

Dear Aiden Shaw,

Unaccustomed as I am to corresponding with poets of any kind, whether kind or unkind, and never having known a novelist, not even Biblically, and notwithstanding the fact that porn stars never brighten my firmament, nevertheless I take this opportunity …

[Yadee Yadee Yadee]

… and am therefore convinced that by pooling our considerable talents, perhaps even rubbing them together, and by mixing passions with metaphors, we might compose such an angelic chorale would bring the very heavens to account. In short, will you make an honest fellow of me? Will you, in a manner of speaking, marry me?

He kissed the envelope with very pretty stamps.

And discovered that love is a waiting game.

It was all of three weeks before the reply came back

Yes.

"Hallelujah!" he ejaculated.

They were destined to live happily and promiscuously ever after.

****

Bernie, with an embarrassment of flowers, caught the bus. Perhaps he could hide the blooms folding the tissue paper so. Or if he held them upside down, thus, the others might think it a bunch of celery. After all, they were all of them off to the mental hospital. They'd probably believe in celery.

He was given instructions. He followed the yellow brick road signs. The ward was snow white. The nurse smiled an off-white smile as she took charge of the flowers. She arranged them in a cracked vase, carelessly, as though they were sticks of celery.

"So how are they treating you?"

"Pills."

"Pills?"

"Yes. Green ones in the morning, and blue ones at night."

"Ah. Pills of a different colour. And what are you in for?"

"Destiny."

"For ever? Surely not for ever!"

"No. For designing destiny. They won't believe I can make things happen. They won't believe I can determine destinies. They say I'm deluded. Irresponsible. Even dangerous."

"Well what did you do?"

"It was the cat next door. You know, the one that came in to get my peaceful doves. I'd feed them crumbs. The next thing that bloody cat would be in. I told the woman. I said I had a strong feeling, in fact I felt sure her cat would meet its destiny the following week."

"And did it?"

"Yes. It did."

"How?"

"I hit it with a spade."

"And have you destined anything else recently?"

"Well yes, as a matter of fact. But I'm not saying what. You wouldn't believe me anyway. Now you could do me a favour Bernie. Would you take this gold ring. Keep it for me. I know that nurse has other ideas. Put it in a safe place where no one will find it. Put it in your underpants perhaps."

"Richard, they're Calvin Kleins …"

"Well give them back."

"…and I don't want dirty verdigris marks. What would people think?"

****

Bernie's eyes had never been good. They had not improved with years. Under a strong magnifying glass he could make out the ring was twenty-two carat and was inscribed

Eternal love. A.S.

Just then the phone rang.

"Bernie? Aidan Shaw. Just in by Qantas. The house is deserted. I'm ringing a few likely numbers. Have you seen my Dick?"

Bernie wasn't sure, couldn't help wondering if that were spelt with a capital 'D'.

And if he were destined to find out.

The Trouble with Ants

Some people believe that ants are stupid. Not so. They are as cunning as church mice. Why do you think mice go to church? Because they know it's a holy place. Get it? Hole? Holy? Mouse holes? Oh never mind.

But ants will go anywhere warm and dry and promising a feed. Take your oven for example. Ants take to ovens like mice to church. If you suspect they have taken to yours, there are various moves you should make.

First, switch on the oven lights every second day, just to determine if your oven has ants. If you detect an ant, count it, no matter where it may be in the house. One ant may not be a disaster. Two spell trouble. They talk to each other, and they have never heard of the word secret.

Two ants are sufficient to start a trail. Follow them, but on tiptoe. If they look around, pretend you are doing the washing-up. If you are not in the habit of washing-up, scratch under your arms. The ants will assume you are more interested in fleas. And they will eventually lead you to the rest of the family, numbering several millions. Ants have a migratory fixation. They believe the world is always better somewhere else. And they are right. Eventually they will decide your oven could be heaven. Now you're for it.

As soon as you discover the ants in the oven, switch off the oven lights. The ants mustn't know that you know. If they see you looking, this will set their antennas working, and start a panic. A stampede of ants is an ugly business.

Then if your kitchen has an anteroom, lock the doors. But make sure to remember where you put the key, just in case you are overwhelmed. It is already too late to check your insurance policy. You will also need a vacuum cleaner.

Next set your oven to maximum high grill fan siren red emergency and switch it on. Stand on the anterior side of the oven. This is where they will be. Select the antipathy setting on your vacuum cleaner. Switch it on. Once the ants have worked out this is not just another hot day at the beach, they will begin to emerge, running. As they do, suck them up.

At this stage, your cover has already been blown, so you can switch on the oven lights. There you will observe egregious panics and alarms and ants fleeing in all directions. See. You were interested in flees.

Soon there will be an avalanche of ants. Some millions may escape. Have handy a pressure pack insect spray. Aim it at the escapees and press button A for Ant. Meanwhile, keep sucking up the rest, but as soon as you have a moment, aim the nozzle at the pressure packed mob. Some of these will have lost concentration and be wandering off. There are jokers in every pack. A rolled up newspaper should see them off the planet. Not *The Times*. Something more modest.

After ten or so minutes, the wriggling and writhing will have ceased. Switch off the oven. Open the door. You will discover the ants well-done and reclining in discrete piles. If you are not an anteater, these too can be sucked up in your vacuum cleaner.

Finally, wipe the inside of the oven with a damp cloth. This will remove the antecedents, the footprints, and all evidence of the massacre you have so cleverly and heartlessly engineered.

However, you will need more than a damp cloth to expunge the details of this dastardly episode from your conscience and memory.

You rotten swine!

The three monkeys

This is the story of the three monkeys.

Once upon a tiny time, there were three monkeys.

Well, one was really a gorilla, but you don't argue with a gorilla.

And they all lived together in Glenthorne Drive, in a little shed behind Oona's house. They were very quiet there, which is unusual for monkeys, but on some still nights, if you listened very carefully, you might hear them munching on bananas - or pineapples.

Early one morning, out walking, they found a credit card in the road. It really belonged to the three giraffes, four doors down, but they didn't care. Well you know what monkeys monkeys are. And they all caught a tram in to Myers to go shopping.

This was their first trip to town. They didn't know where things were, nor what was up, nor what was down. So they asked the girl at the Information Counter.

"Are you the girl with information?" they asked.

"Yes" she smiled, sweetly. She used to work in the Sweets Department you see. Until she was promoted when she heard some gossip about Mr. …
But that's another story. "Yes" she smiled. "It's printed on my badge you see."
And she pointed to her plastic badge with the safety pin, pinned onto her left … chest. And it said - in quite large print, big enough for monkeys to read -

MISS INFORMATION.

"Well. She must know," said the gorilla.

"She probably knows," said the orang-utan.
"I think she knows," said the spider monkey.

"Where is the Gorilla Department?" demanded the gorilla.
"There is no Gorilla Department," she answered, pertly, but with a sweet smile.
"And the Orange Fizz Department," said the orang-utan.
"And the Spider Monkey Spider Web Department," said the spider monkey.
"No. No. None of those," answered the thin-lipped information lady, rather less sweetly.

"But I need a new gorilla suit" said the gorilla.
"And I'm desperate for an orange fizz" said the orang-utan.
"And I need a new spider monkey spider web" said the spider monkey.
"Whatever for?" asked Miss Thin Lips.
"For catching flying bananas," said the spider monkey
"Bananas don't fly, so there."
"Well. Pineapples then, and I need it today."

The information lady took a very deep breath, swelling with impatience, as there was by now quite a long queue of questioning customers waiting behind the monkeys. And she was beginning to wish she were safely back in the Sweet Department.

"I am led to believe you are a pack of troublesome monkeys. You should all be in a cage - a cagefull of monkeys."

Well did this get their monkey up!

"What? What? We're not from the zoo you know," said the gorilla.
"We're private citizens," said the orang-utan.
"And what's more, we're telling on you," said the spider monkey.

"I shall have to call the Manager," said the information lady, bitterly.

"What will you call him?" said the gorilla.
"Boofhead?" suggested the orang-utan.
"Bozo," suggested the spider monkey.

"I shall call him at once," she replied.

"At Once," yelled the gorilla.
"At Once," shrieked the orang-utan.
"At Once," shrilled the spider monkey.

"Coming," shouted a voice from above, and Mr Atwunce, dressed in a gorilla suit, came charging down the up-escalator, knocking mothers and babies and grandmothers and grand-babies flying this way and that in his desperate haste to get to the bottom of this very rowdy mystery on the ground floor.

"Now what's the problem?" he panted, arriving, and looking perplexed at a baby's bottle seemed to be caught in his gorilla suit.

"These monkey gentlemen …" began Miss Bitterness. But she was interrupted by the gorilla, who was no gentleman.

"Why are you wearing, and where did you get that gorilla suit?" he demanded of Mr Atwunce.

"Well from our overstocked Gorilla Department of course. And they're on special. And I'm special. So I put one on."

"But there is no Gorilla Department," sobbed the disintegrating information lady.

"Oh yes there is. Oh yes indeed, indeed there is indeed. Just opened. Ten minutes ago. Brand new. Everything on sale."

"And an Orange Fizz Department?" murmured the orang-utan, hopefully.

"That too. Yes indeed. That too."

"And a Spider Monkey Spider Web Department?" whispered the astonished Spider Monkey.

"Oh yes indeed. We cater for all and sundry at Myers. We even cater for monkeys. Walk this way Gentlemen. Follow me!" as he minced up the up escalator, the three monkeys aping his mince behind, with a "'Scuse us! Make way. Careful now." to the mothers and babies and grand-mothers and grand-babies still scattered about, wondering what had so recently hit them.

And do you know, they were never seen again, the gorilla, and the orang-utan, and the spider monkey, nor for that matter, Mr. Atwunce, not in the Gorilla Department, not in the Orange Fizz Department, and not in the Spider Monkey Spider Web Department. But Miss Information went back to Sweets saying she was over-stressed.

"She was always over-dressed," hissed Miss Birthday Cakes. But that's another story.

"Whatever happened to the monkeys?" you might ask. Well the midnight cleaners say they have from time to time heard quite a kerfuffle and crunch in the Nut Department, and monkey chuckles in the Sports Department, and simian sniggers and cheerful chatter in Fun and Games.

But I really think they all caught a tram back to Oona's, for on some still nights, if you listen very carefully, you can hear some contented snoring and snuffles and occasional giggles from the little shed at the back of her house. And sometimes a hissed command

"Get out of that Atwunce."

Well there we are
The book is done.

I hope you had
A heap of fun.

www.ingramcontent.com/pod-product-compliance
Lightning Source LLC
Chambersburg PA
CBHW060344080526
44584CB00013B/909